THE SILK ROADS

THE SILK ROADS

ROWAN EVERHART

CONTENTS

CHAPTER 1

Introduction

The conventional narrative surrounding the Silk Roads has long been held in high regard by historians, scholars, and the general public alike. However, such an unreserved acceptance of the established storyline, which has been perpetuated for decades, if not centuries, is not only disrespectful to the numerous scholars and colleagues whose work challenges this orthodoxy but also fuels unnecessary academic rivalry and jealousy. Indeed, many modern non-scholars, including most publishers, remain infatuated with the old story. Surprisingly, even some ancient historians have begun to buy into an outdated, textbook version of history, often influenced by misleading perspectives propagated by priests and other biased sources.

Several enlightened scholars have recently asserted that one of humanity's most enduring tendencies is the belief that the truly golden years are the ones we are currently living through. This nostalgic fallacy skews our understanding of the past, leading to a romanticized and often inaccurate portrayal of historical events.

My book aims to respond to what I see as deeply erroneous and misleading literature concerning the nature of Mediterranean-Asian exchanges between 50 BC and AD 800. Much of what I was taught at university about how these trade networks operated, why they emerged, how they evolved, the types of individuals involved in these journeys, and the goods they transported, is fundamentally flawed. These teachings are based on a narrow interpretation of sources that are both ideologically biased and historically inaccurate.

I propose to write a comprehensive history of what I call "trans-Eurasian trade networks," a term that better reflects the intricate web of routes known colloquially as the "Silk Roads." The plural form "Silk Roads" has gained popularity in recent years, acknowledging that in pre-modern times, there wasn't a single route but multiple pathways connecting East Asia to the Mediterranean and the Indian Ocean. These were the arteries through which almost all significant exchanges of value flowed. Despite this complexity, the allure of the Spice and Silk Roads continues to captivate historians and enthusiasts alike.

Through this work, I aim to shed light on the true nature of these ancient trade networks, debunking myths and presenting a more nuanced and accurate picture of how these connections shaped the world. By examining a broader range of sources and perspectives, I hope to contribute to a more comprehensive understanding of our shared history.

CHAPTER 2

The Origins of the Silk Roads

The Silk Roads were a sprawling network of trade routes that facilitated the exchange of goods, culture, and ideas between the East and the West. These routes saw a vast array of items transported across Afro-Eurasia, creating a complex tapestry of commerce and interaction. Roman glass, golden sculptures, Greek wines, Egyptian cotton, Indian spices, and African ivory were among the myriad goods that changed hands numerous times before reaching their final destinations.

From the earliest days of agriculture and animal husbandry, communities that successfully accumulated significant surpluses sought various ways to reinvest their wealth. One prominent approach was to finance trading networks that not only brought rare and exotic items but also opened new markets for local and regional products. This economic reinvestment played a pivotal role in the development and expansion of trade routes.

When I first delved into the history of these exchanges, particularly in China and beyond, two critical questions emerged: how did these trade routes impact the lives of the people who lived alongside them, and how did they shape the course of history? These questions remain central to the narrative of this book.

Firstly, there is the nature of the trade routes themselves. The term "Silk Roads" was coined in 1877 by the German geographer Ferdinand von Richthofen. He used it to describe the network of caravan tracks and sea lanes that transported silk from China to the Roman Empire. However, I contend that the term "Silk Roads" and all that it implies is fundamentally misleading.

The Silk Roads were not merely pathways for the exchange of silk; they were dynamic arteries of trade that carried a plethora of goods, ideas, and cultural influences. The term "Silk Roads" oversimplifies the multifaceted nature of these routes. In reality, they encompassed a wide range of interconnected pathways that facilitated the exchange of diverse commodities and cultural interactions across vast distances.

These trade routes were vital in shaping the economic, social, and cultural landscapes of the regions they traversed. They enabled the flow of not just goods but also knowledge, technology, and religious beliefs. The impact of these exchanges on local communities was profound, influencing their way of life, their economies, and their interactions with neighboring regions.

As we explore the origins and evolution of these trans-Eurasian trade networks, it becomes clear that the Silk Roads were far more than just trade routes for silk. They were the lifelines of civilizations, fostering connections and exchanges that would shape the course of history. Through this book, I aim to provide a deeper understanding of these ancient networks, shedding light on their true nature and significance.

CHAPTER 3

The Silk Roads in Ancient Times

The Silk Roads, a sprawling network of trade routes, facilitated the exchange of a diverse range of products between East and West. From Roman glass to golden sculptures, Greek wines to Egyptian cotton, Indian spices to African ivory, a kaleidoscope of goods traversed these routes. These products often changed hands multiple times, creating a vibrant tapestry of commerce and cultural interaction.

The early traces of these trade routes can be observed in the wagon tracks that later evolved into main north-south trunk routes. These included the Italian Silk Road, the Peninsular Silk Road, the Indian 'Merchants' Road', four lines in India, and one in Malaysia. These routes foreshadowed Europe's grand voyages of discovery, connecting continents and civilizations long before the age of exploration.

Religious ideas and beliefs also followed these tracks, carried by wandering dignitaries, often referred to in Chinese as 'yi-wang-piao' or 'reverend wandering'. This term, associated with the figure of Zoroaster, highlights the role of these routes in disseminating spiritual and philosophical thoughts across vast distances. The Greeks, during their interactions with the steppe nomads, adopted the horse and chariot arts, further illustrating the cultural exchanges facilitated by these ancient highways.

The phrase 'Silk Roads' encapsulates the significant role these trade routes played in antiquity. However, it was not just silk that was traded along these paths. The Chinese developed the art of sericulture as early as the fourth millennium BCE, but access to Chinese silk became more widespread from the Han Dynasty (206 BCE-220 CE) onwards. This valuable commodity was just one of many that moved along these routes.

Across the heartlands of Afro-Eurasia, from the Mediterranean to East Asia, a long line of interconnected great cities and markets offered an enticing array of products. These markets were bustling hubs where traders and merchants from various cultures and backgrounds came together. The sea, though named singularly, encompassed multiple routes leading to India. One such route landed at the indigo-producing area, highlighting the intricate web of pathways that traders navigated.

Indigo, prized for its deep blue dye, was not initially available for sea transport further east. However, the heavily utilized overland networks provided more opportunities for trade at key nodes such as Taxila, a city that was a significant trading hub and crossroads for various cultures. Taxila, known for its encounters with both Darius's Greeks and Alexander's Macedonians, served as a vital point in the exchange of goods and ideas.

These ancient trade routes were more than just pathways for commerce; they were conduits for cultural, technological, and intellectual exchanges that shaped the civilizations they connected. Through this examination, we can begin to appreciate the profound impact of the Silk Roads on the development of human history.

CHAPTER 4

The Impact of the Silk Roads on Trade

The near synchronous formation of these new ocean-land trade routes, both by land and sea, heralded a new era of sustained prosperity. Human population growth, always correlated with a strong and dynamic economy, surged as a result of these developments. More intensive land usage, including the conversion of pastoral lands and forests into farmlands, and the establishment of numerous trading depots, flourished. Overuse of previously feral lands was driven by increased trading opportunities, bringing them into productive use. This period can be seen as an ancient "modern moment" in the Old World, predating the "discovery" of the New World and the industrialization of agriculture.

If we are to measure the past by its legacy, then this era stands as a testament to economic resilience and growth. Such a perspective offers a consoling correction to contemporary worries about economic downturns. With the benefit of hindsight, recessions and depressions may not seem as dire when compared to the robust economic activity of this historical period.

The Silk Roads significantly influenced trade and economic activity, much like the movement of Eurasians did for the cultural integration and miscegenation of various peoples. The Eurasian continent, home to numerous trading zones extending in all directions, required an economic rationale to integrate the new inroads provided by overland trading routes. Well-used maritime trading routes connected the Indian, Pacific, and Atlantic Oceans, forming the first truly global trading network. This network, which included between 1,000 and 20,000 ocean-going ships, operated in a trading world that had remained largely unchanged for over 2,000 years.

Along the Silk Roads, multiple routes converged at local markets, providing direct access to previously isolated areas. These markets became bustling hubs where traders from diverse regions interacted, exchanged goods, and shared cultural practices. The convergence of these roads facilitated the integration of new trading zones, enhancing economic activity and promoting cultural exchanges.

The impact of the Silk Roads extended beyond mere commerce. They were conduits for the exchange of ideas, technologies, and religions, influencing the development of the societies they connected. The trade routes fostered economic interdependence, leading to a more integrated and interconnected world. As a result, the Silk Roads played a crucial role in shaping the economic, social, and cultural landscapes of the regions they touched.

In conclusion, the Silk Roads were instrumental in driving economic growth and cultural integration in the ancient world. Their legacy is a testament to the power of trade and exchange in shaping human history. By understanding the impact of these trade routes, we can gain valuable insights into the processes that have shaped our modern world.

CHAPTER 5

Cultural Exchange along the Silk Roads

Evidence of cultural exchange along the Silk Roads is vast and varied, suggesting the existence of a complex network of maritime and overland institutions that facilitated the movement of goods and ideas. This chapter explores the spread of languages, artifacts, and cultural goods, shedding light on the intricate web of connections that characterized these ancient trade routes.

Analyzing the spread of languages found in coins and Western Mediterranean Bronze Age (MBA) objects reveals that network impacts were already present during the period commonly referred to as "Before Common Era" (BCE). For instance, 11 Western malachite objects have been discovered in the East of Peninsular Arabia, indicating early trade interactions. Moreover, some objects composed of both foreign and domestic substances were developed prematurely during the Roman period. These malachite artifacts, combined with evidence of trade in black shiny stones and ornaments from the Divino Serbia tradition, highlight the diversity of goods exchanged across these networks.

The range of Eastern cultural goods found in the Roman world suggests that Western markets had a significant appetite for these exotic items. By analyzing the distribution of such finds, we can gain insights into the networks through which they spread. Before the rise of the Roman Empire, quartz was transported between urban systems, with the Persians exchanging goods with Babylon. Glass and copper later became key commodities in these exchanges. The pearls and textiles of South India were also highly prized and exported extensively.

Trade across the Arabian Sea, particularly with South India, predates Roman commerce, indicating that these networks were well-established long before the Roman Republic or Empire. The maritime routes that connected the Indian, Persian, and Roman worlds were crucial for the exchange of goods and cultural practices. These routes enabled the flow of diverse commodities, including the highly valued indigo dye, which was transported overland before being accessible for sea transport further east.

The impact of these cultural exchanges extended beyond the mere transfer of goods. They facilitated the spread of ideas, technologies, and religious beliefs, contributing to the cultural richness and diversity of the regions connected by the Silk Roads. The integration of new trading zones into these networks necessitated an economic rationale that promoted efficiency and effectiveness, leading to a more interconnected and interdependent world.

In conclusion, the cultural exchange along the Silk Roads was instrumental in shaping the societies of ancient times. The movement of goods and ideas across these vast distances fostered a dynamic and interconnected world, enriching the cultural landscapes of the regions involved. By examining the evidence of these exchanges, we gain a deeper understanding of the profound impact of the Silk Roads on the development of human civilization.

CHAPTER 6

The Silk Roads and the Spread of Ideas

The Silk Roads were not just channels for the exchange of goods; they were also vital conduits for the dissemination of ideas, culture, and technology. This chapter explores how these ancient trade routes facilitated cultural exchange and intellectual growth across civilizations.

The medieval Chinese were deeply concerned about their interactions with foreign cultures. The Ministry for Rites, for example, feared that China had been reduced to merely receiving gifts from others, rather than being the source of cultural influence. They lamented that "Our advanced music, our court dances, our silk and our fine wares, and our flora and fauna, our fruits and seed are being sent to the foreign countries of every quarter of the world." This anxiety over cultural exchange and its potential to undermine Chinese superiority was echoed centuries later by the Manchus. By the 19th century, they perceived themselves as victims of outside influence. Empress Dowager Cixi sought to convince her court that while Western technologies might be suitable for other Chinese people, her divine essence and regency for her son, Emperor Tongzhi, made her an exception. She believed it would be fatal for her to follow the example of mere mortals.

Travelers along the Silk Roads, such as Marco Polo, had ample time to observe and reflect on the cultures they encountered. The long distances they traversed allowed them to ponder the fate of the people living along these routes. Many of the sites between Europe and China had once been major population centers. In the Western half of the Roman Empire, followed by the various realms known as the Holy Roman Empire, sub-Roman Britain, and medieval France and the Low Countries, many cities had become ghost towns, abandoned by the descendants of their Roman creators. However, the land around their ruined walls often remained largely untouched since the days of the Romans or even the Neolithic farmers who first settled these regions when the Mediterranean world was an economic and cultural powerhouse.

The Silk Roads played a crucial role in the spread of ideas and technological innovations. For instance, the transmission of knowledge about papermaking from China to the Islamic world and then to Europe revolutionized communication and record-keeping. Similarly, the spread of gunpowder technology had a profound impact on military tactics and weaponry across Eurasia.

Religious ideas also traveled along these routes. Buddhism spread from India to East Asia, while Nestorian Christianity made its way to China. The exchange of religious beliefs and practices fostered a rich tapestry of spiritual diversity along the Silk Roads.

The influence of these trade routes extended beyond the exchange of tangible goods. They facilitated the spread of intellectual ideas, artistic styles, and cultural practices. This dynamic interchange enriched the civilizations connected by the Silk Roads, fostering a vibrant and interconnected world.

In conclusion, the Silk Roads were instrumental in the spread of ideas, culture, and technology. They provided a platform for the exchange of knowledge and innovations that shaped the development of societies across Eurasia. By understanding the cultural impact of these trade routes, we can appreciate their role in shaping the intellectual and cultural landscapes of the ancient world.

CHAPTER 7

The Silk Roads and the Development of Cities

The Silk Roads were instrumental in connecting not just tangible goods, but also ideas, knowledge, and cultural values. The cargo that traversed these routes often comprised luxury items, not merely for physical adornment, but for enriching the soul. These included mathematical inquiries into the nature of truth and goodness, spiritual quests for justice, artistic endeavors for beauty, and ethical reflections on compassion. The intellectual curiosity and cultural aspirations of people were not confined by physical boundaries. In their essence, they were always navigating various Silk Roads, seeking any vessel of thought that could offer divine or noble guidance.

As elite travelers journeyed along the Silk Roads, their interactions facilitated the exchange of knowledge from the Indo-Mediterranean lands to the heart of Asia and eventually to Han and post-Han China. This cross-cultural exchange enriched societies and fostered a shared intellectual heritage.

Before delving into the development of resupply cities along these routes, it is crucial to recognize the significant resources that the Silk Roads' caravans transported. While geographical challenges such as mountains, desiccation, and disease undoubtedly shaped the Silk Road narrative, the diverse array of goods carried by these caravans was even more pivotal. The Silk Roads, or perhaps more aptly, the "Nano Silk Roads," served not merely as trade conduits but also as connectors of luxury goods and repositories of knowledge. They linked the exquisite beads of commerce with the enduring towers of intellectual pursuit.

The air of learning and the collective wisdom of those engaged in these exchanges were as vital as the material goods themselves. The metaphorical winds of philosophy and knowledge propelled the arts and sciences, much like camels that communicated through the shadows cast by their encounters. This exchange of ideas was crucial to the development and flourishing of cities along the Silk Roads.

Cities such as Samarkand, Bukhara, and Chang'an became bustling hubs of trade and culture, drawing merchants, scholars, and travelers from far and wide. These cities were not just resupply points for caravans but vibrant centers of learning and cultural exchange. Libraries, schools, and marketplaces thrived, creating a dynamic environment where ideas and goods flowed freely. The architectural and cultural legacies of these cities bear testament to the profound impact of the Silk Roads on urban development.

The convergence of different cultures in these cities led to the blending of artistic styles, culinary traditions, and religious practices. This cultural fusion enriched the lives of the inhabitants and left an indelible mark on the urban landscape. The cities along the Silk Roads became melting pots of diversity, fostering innovation and creativity.

In conclusion, the Silk Roads played a crucial role in the development of cities, not only by facilitating trade but also by serving as channels for the exchange of ideas and knowledge. The intellectual and cultural exchanges along these routes contributed significantly to the growth and prosperity of urban centers, leaving a lasting legacy that continues to inspire and captivate.

CHAPTER 8

The Silk Roads and the Rise of Empires

The Silk Roads were deeply intertwined with the rise of several prominent empires, including the Romans and the Parthians. These ancient trade routes facilitated not only the exchange of goods but also the flow of ideas, technologies, and cultural practices, contributing significantly to the growth and expansion of these empires. The Afroeurasian supercontinent, particularly its core regions, became interconnected to an extent that it functioned almost like a single, albeit vast, subcontinent.

As the Iron Age came to a close, the emergence of the Silk Roads supported the birth of new empires and marked the transition to the Classical Age. This period saw the continued dominance of the Hellenes and the rise of several Eastern empires. The first half of Peter Frankopan's "The Silk Roads" ostensibly chronicles the history of these ancient trade routes. However, it becomes apparent that the book is more about the shift of global influence from the Mediterranean to the Pacific. Despite this focus, the ancient Silk Roads remain a central theme throughout the work, highlighting their enduring influence and importance.

The book's narrative spans the development of the seven empires of eastern Antiquity, which the author refers to as "aros" to juxtapose them with their Western counterparts. These empires played crucial roles in shaping the cultural and economic landscape of the ancient world. However, the omission of China proper from Frankopan's account is a notable oversight. Given China's significant role in the Silk Roads until the rise of the Caliphate, it is impossible to write a comprehensive history of these trade routes without acknowledging China's contributions.

The Silk Roads not only facilitated trade but also the exchange of knowledge and cultural practices, which were crucial for the development of empires. For instance, the Romans benefited from the flow of luxury goods, such as silk and spices, which were highly prized in their society. Similarly, the Parthians controlled key segments of the Silk Roads, which enabled them to exert influence over the trade networks and enrich their empire.

The integration of the Afroeurasian supercontinent through the Silk Roads laid the foundation for sustained economic growth and cultural exchange. These trade routes connected the great cities and markets of the region, fostering a dynamic environment where goods, ideas, and technologies flowed freely. The rise of empires along the Silk Roads was not just a consequence of economic prosperity but also a result of the rich cultural and intellectual exchanges that these routes facilitated.

In conclusion, the Silk Roads were instrumental in the rise of several ancient empires. Their legacy is evident in the cultural and economic developments that shaped the ancient world. By understanding the impact of these trade routes, we can gain valuable insights into the processes that have influenced the course of history.

CHAPTER 9

The Silk Roads and the Transmission of Knowledge

The Silk Roads functioned as the primary "information super-highways" of the ancient world, facilitating the exchange of knowledge, culture, and technology across vast distances. The network's capillary nature, supported by itinerant peddlers, merchant ambassadors, and sea captains, was crucial to the ongoing reliability of these trade and information networks. As long as merchants felt protected, they traversed not only the short sections of the Silk Roads but also the comparatively more secure stretch of the Indian Ocean, interconnecting the two networks. The circulation of information was as vital as the goods being traded, binding ancient travelers together in a shared intellectual and cultural exchange.

Much like railways and telegraphic lines that would later weave networks across political boundaries, the Silk Roads fostered the exchange of thought and knowledge between the clusters of human populations connected by these intercontinental nodes. This exchange was fundamental to the transmission of knowledge and cultural practices along the Silk Roads.

Antoninus Pius, Roman emperor from 138 to 161 CE, epitomized the significance of these routes. He expressed his delight at the completion of a new, straight stretch of road from Antioch to Chalcis in Syria, which facilitated his journey from Rome overland into the Far East. This road, predating the reign of Hadrian, exemplified the Roman Empire's commitment to connecting distant provinces through well-constructed infrastructure. Once this overland route brought emperors into the Near Eastern provinces, soldiers and other members of the imperial entourage could anticipate the remainder of their journey along the Mediterranean coast, across the Aegean, and around the Bosphorus. A small number of ships could be transshipped by portagers across the land divide to the Black Sea upon reaching Sinope.

The interconnectedness fostered by the Silk Roads enabled the spread of technological innovations and intellectual ideas. For example, the knowledge of papermaking, which originated in China, spread to the Islamic world and eventually reached Europe, revolutionizing communication and record-keeping. Similarly, the transmission of gunpowder technology had a profound impact on military tactics and weaponry across Eurasia.

Religious ideas also traveled along these routes. Buddhism spread from India to East Asia, while Nestorian Christianity made its way to China. These religious exchanges contributed to the rich tapestry of spiritual diversity along the Silk Roads, enhancing the cultural landscapes of the regions involved.

In addition to religious and technological exchanges, artistic and literary ideas flourished along the Silk Roads. Artisans and scholars shared their techniques and knowledge, leading to a cross-fertilization of artistic styles and intellectual thought. This cultural synthesis enriched the societies connected by the Silk Roads, fostering a dynamic and interconnected world.

In conclusion, the Silk Roads were instrumental in the transmission of knowledge, culture, and technology. They served as conduits for the exchange of ideas and innovations that shaped the development of human civilization. By understanding the impact of these trade routes, we can appreciate their role in creating a vibrant and interconnected ancient world.

CHAPTER 10

The Silk Roads and the Exchange of Goods

The exchange of goods along the Silk Roads was fraught with numerous challenges and dangers. Maintaining enough food and water for both humans and animals was a significant economic difficulty. For instance, the forty-day journey from Dunhuang to Anxi required careful planning and ample supplies of food and water. Some Roman caravans in the Levant carried water in glazed pottery jugs known as amphorae. However, these jugs were heavy, with each gallon weighing approximately sixteen pounds. A donkey, capable of carrying about 225 pounds at most, could be significantly burdened by the weight of these jugs, especially in conditions of intense heat and light.

In addition to the economic difficulties, there were physical dangers. Caravans faced environmental hardships, such as the risk of getting lost in sandstorms or succumbing to extreme heat. They were also vulnerable to attacks by robbers who, while sometimes offering protection, would not do so without a hefty price.

Deserts, which caravans often traversed, presented their own unique challenges, primarily water scarcity and the threat of bandits. The process of crossing deserts, such as the journey from Dunhuang to Anxi, was comparable to the way merchant ships navigated the Indian Ocean. Caravans frequently utilized the Qaidam Depression and other salt flats to execute complicated north-south switchbacks across the Tengger Desert. These strategic routes were essential for survival in such harsh environments.

The Silk Roads also served as conduits for a diverse array of goods. Merchants transported luxury items, such as silk, spices, precious stones, and exotic animals, which were highly prized in different parts of the world. Additionally, everyday commodities like grains, textiles, and metals were traded, supporting the economic stability of the regions connected by these routes.

In 2000, German adventurer Gerllard Haussler retraced the ancient route to India using a mountain bike to personally test the Macedonian satrap Altfluxars' claim from 325 BCE. Altfluxars had asserted that goods could be easily transported from India to Bactra by donkey, from the mouth of the Indus to the Amu Darya. Haussler's journey underscored the enduring significance of these ancient trade routes and the remarkable resilience of those who traversed them.

Despite the numerous challenges, the Silk Roads facilitated the exchange of goods on an unprecedented scale, connecting diverse cultures and economies across vast distances. The caravans that traveled these routes not only transported valuable commodities but also fostered economic interdependence and cultural exchange.

In conclusion, the Silk Roads were instrumental in the exchange of goods, overcoming significant economic and physical challenges. The movement of commodities along these routes played a crucial role in shaping the economic and cultural landscapes of the ancient world. By examining the intricacies of these trade networks, we gain a deeper understanding of their impact on global history.

CHAPTER 11

The Silk Roads and the Silk Industry

The Silk Roads were not just trade routes for finished goods, but also pathways for the transmission of technological knowledge and production techniques, such as those involved in traditional silk production. Ancient techniques for the rearing and breeding of silkworms, whose cocoons provided the thread for silk fabric, have been documented in historical records. The production process involved several stages, including the rearing of silkworms, the harvesting of cocoons, and the extraction and weaving of silk threads into fabric.

Once produced, these swaths of silk cloth were bleached, stored, and traded along the expansive network of the Silk Roads. Initially, the trade of silk began within China and extended to the western regions, gradually expanding to cover much of the ancient world. This trade continued until the fall of the Roman Empire. The Byzantine Empire later revived these practices, albeit briefly, by reconquering key sections of the Silk Roads. During the Middle Ages, the Arab Empire further expanded these trade networks, integrating various cultural and technological traditions into the lands it conquered.

The historical significance of the Silk Roads lies not only in the exchange of merchandise but also in the interregional exchanges of ideas, beliefs, technologies, fashions, artistic styles, and other cultural phenomena. These exchanges can be more readily grasped today, as they provide insight into the ancient practices of interregional transfers and exchanges between widely separated technological milieus. Understanding these historical exchanges is significant for comprehending the foundations of our contemporary world.

Traditional historical methods have been employed to produce a logical framework for comparative historical analysis, allowing us to examine the exchange of goods and the formation of specific regional industries along the Silk Roads. For example, the silk industry, which was deeply rooted in China, spread to other regions through these networks. This spread was facilitated by the movement of artisans, traders, and technological knowledge.

In addition to the production and trade of silk, the Silk Roads facilitated the exchange of other luxury items, such as spices, precious stones, and exotic animals. These goods were highly prized in different parts of the world and contributed to the economic prosperity of the regions connected by the Silk Roads.

The circulation of knowledge and technology along the Silk Roads also led to significant advancements in various fields. For instance, the techniques for papermaking and gunpowder production, which originated in China, spread to other parts of the world through these trade routes. Similarly, artistic and architectural styles were exchanged, leading to a rich cultural synthesis.

In conclusion, the Silk Roads played a crucial role in the development and dissemination of the silk industry. They served as channels for the exchange of goods, knowledge, and cultural practices, shaping the economic and cultural landscapes of the ancient world. By examining the intricacies of these trade networks, we gain a deeper understanding of their impact on global history and the development of our contemporary era.

CHAPTER 12

The Decline of the Silk Roads

The Silk Roads did not simply vanish with the decline of the Roman Empire; instead, they transitioned into a more complex post-Roman business mode. This continued mobility of goods, even during severe periods of crisis, has been praised by Orientalists in the nineteenth century. Assets, whether goods or information, found different pathways and means of distribution over both short and long periods. The so-called Silk Roads experienced shifts rather than a complete breakdown, maintaining essential links between Rome and its far-Eastern suppliers.

Despite these transitions, the interconnectedness of Rome and its distant suppliers persisted through various means. For instance, wine-loaded donkeys, overseen by polite, albeit inebriated, Sassanian courtier-retailers, traversed these ancient routes. Such exchanges highlight the continued demand for Chinese silk, even as smallholder villages in regions like Oppian, close to the Roman city named after the Assyrian goddess Sibisis, craved this luxurious fabric.

The relationship between new superpower China and declining superpower Rome was complex but manageable. The rise of new faiths also intersected with the teachings of the Silk Roads. In the desert metropolis of Mecca, the new faith of Islam found a harmonious fit with the trade networks of the Silk Roads. Muhammad, much like Jesus, acknowledged the existence of these trade networks in his teachings. He imposed payments on goods that supported his new faith, reflecting the economic underpinnings of religious practices.

The ancient connectivity celebrated by Procopius in his sixth-century hymns echoed the early connectivity of the Roman Empire. These hymns highlighted the continuity of the fabled trade saga, despite ancient animosities. Prejudices about oriental or occidental 'endangerers of piety' and 'slanderers of respectable societies' still abound, complicating modern analyses of religious controversies among sellers and buyers' co-religionists.

As the Silk Roads adapted to new political and economic realities, they continued to facilitate the exchange of goods and ideas. While the Roman Empire declined, new powers such as the Byzantine Empire and the Islamic Caliphate rose, inheriting and expanding the trade networks. These new empires maintained the flow of goods, knowledge, and culture along the Silk Roads, ensuring their continued relevance.

In conclusion, the decline of the Silk Roads was not a straightforward collapse but a transformation into a more complex and adaptive trade network. The routes persisted through changing political landscapes, continuing to connect distant regions and facilitate the exchange of goods and ideas. By examining this period of transition, we can better understand the resilience and adaptability of these ancient trade routes.

CHAPTER 13

The Legacy of the Silk Roads

The legacy of the Silk Roads is vast and multifaceted, touching various aspects of human civilization. Even as ultranationalism posed challenges, workers in sectors such as hospitality, restoration, and law enforcement faced the monumental task of maintaining the heritage sites along these ancient trade routes. Cities like Samarkand, once hubs of cultural and economic activity, grappled with the impacts of modernization, conflict, and neglect.

The task of rehabilitating a city that has been devastated by conflict and time is daunting. Can a city that has been plowed under, tortured, shelled, and left to decay ever regain its former glory? The answer lies in the resilience of human spirit and the enduring legacy of the Silk Roads. The conventions and laws of human nature that govern such rehabilitation efforts are rooted in a shared sense of history, culture, and a commitment to preserving the past for future generations.

Despite multiple invasions and the repeated destruction of the physical infrastructure of the trade networks, the legacy of the Silk Roads persisted through the people and technologies they connected. The trade networks, which initially facilitated the exchange of luxury goods, evolved to become vital conduits for the transmission of technology and knowledge. These exchanges included religious beliefs, scientific discoveries, craft techniques, art, and alphabets, which were passed along the routes.

One of the most significant relay stations for these exchanges was Samarkand. The city, renowned in the West for its cultural richness, became a symbol of the Silk Roads' enduring legacy. The call of "Oh, it's time I saw Samarkand" echoed among those who admired the city's historical and cultural significance. The city, long hidden from the eyes of the world, began to experience a cultural renaissance. Painters, scientists, poets, novelists, historians, travelers, and scholars from every class and nation flocked to Samarkand, seeking to uncover and celebrate its storied past.

Samarkand's legacy is reflected in the things, dreams, and music of mankind. The city's cultural epiphany was marked by the reawakening of interest in its monuments, which had endured the test of time. The efforts of these visitors and scholars to restore and celebrate Samarkand's heritage symbolized the broader legacy of the Silk Roads—a legacy that transcended physical borders and historical epochs.

The Silk Roads not only facilitated trade but also fostered a dynamic exchange of ideas and cultures that shaped the development of civilizations. This legacy continues to resonate in the modern world, as we strive to preserve and honor the historical and cultural achievements of the past. The resilience of cities like Samarkand stands as a testament to the enduring influence of the Silk Roads.

In conclusion, the legacy of the Silk Roads is a testament to the power of cultural exchange and the resilience of human civilization. Despite the challenges and adversities faced by the cities along these routes, their enduring legacy continues to inspire and captivate. By understanding and preserving this legacy, we can honor the rich tapestry of human history that the Silk Roads represent.

CHAPTER 14

The Revival of the Silk Roads in the Modern Era

The exploration of Central Asia in the modern era owes much to pioneering figures such as the French geographer Pellegrino Strobel (1851-1932). Strobel, who approached Tashkent in 1877, was among the first Europeans to recognize the immense economic potential of Central Asia, not only for Russia but also for Britain and France. His work can be compared to that of the contemporary American geo-strategist Alfred T. Mahan, who, during the same period, identified the control of major communication routes as the key to global dominance. While Mahan focused on the strategic implications of Russian actions in the Pacific for the United States, Strobel was more concerned with the impact of the Treaty of Paris on the Franco-Russian alliance and Sino-Russian relations.

The interest of Russian and European scholars in Central Asia was further fueled by the geopolitical competition known as the Great Game. The agreement signed between Russia and Afghanistan in 1873, and renewed in 1879 under different terms, aimed not only to expand the Russian Empire but also to promote trade and "civilization" in the region. This increased accessibility led to the foundation of the Russian Society of Historical and Philological Studies of the Persian, Turkish, and Tatar Countries in the 1880s. The society, led by Barthold, a pioneering president employed by the Russian ministry of war, played a significant role in fostering scholarly interest in Central Asia.

From the 1860s onward, private expeditions to Central Asia were undertaken by notable figures such as the Swedish explorer Sven Hedin, and the Englishmen Sir Francis Clements and Sir Aurel Stein. These expeditions, often funded by wealthy patrons like the Duke of Loubat, sought to uncover the rich history and cultural heritage of the region. Collectors and copyists were hired to document and preserve the findings, contributing to a growing body of knowledge about Central Asia.

The revival of interest in the Silk Roads during the modern era was driven by a recognition of the region's historical significance and economic potential. The exploration and documentation of Central Asia revealed the enduring legacy of the Silk Roads and their role in shaping the economic and cultural landscapes of the past.

In the contemporary context, the concept of the Silk Roads has been revived through initiatives such as China's Belt and Road Initiative (BRI). This ambitious project aims to enhance connectivity and cooperation across Eurasia, mirroring the ancient Silk Roads' role in facilitating trade and cultural exchange. The BRI seeks to build infrastructure, promote economic development, and foster international collaboration, echoing the goals of the ancient trade networks.

The modern revival of the Silk Roads highlights the continued relevance of these historic routes in fostering global connections. By investing in infrastructure and promoting cross-border cooperation, contemporary initiatives aim to create a more interconnected and prosperous world.

In conclusion, the revival of the Silk Roads in the modern era underscores the enduring significance of these ancient trade routes. The exploration and documentation of Central Asia in the 19th and early 20th centuries laid the groundwork for contemporary efforts to enhance connectivity and cooperation across Eurasia. By understanding the legacy of the Silk Roads, we can appreciate their ongoing impact on global history and their potential to shape the future.

CHAPTER 15

The Silk Roads and Globalization

The concept of the "Silk Roads" has been revived in modern political discourse, symbolizing a desire for global connectivity and enhanced communication links. This ancient network of trade routes has become a powerful metaphor for efforts to counter isolationism and promote cosmopolitan values. Modern political theorists and politicians appeal to the Silk Roads to underscore their global ambitions, whether practical, symbolic, or ideological. They seek a cosmopolitan-like validation for their efforts to globalize the spaces connected by these ancient routes.

One of the most pertinent debates concerning the Silk Roads in the present era centers on their meaning for globalization. The Silk Roads were historically significant for facilitating trade, cultural exchange, and the spread of ideas across vast distances. Today, they are often invoked to highlight the importance of global connectivity in an increasingly interconnected world.

This is not the first age to experience rapid economic, social, and political changes with far-reaching consequences for human societies and the natural environment. However, it is the first era in human history to witness such phenomena on an extraordinarily rapid and broad scale, characterized by unprecedented intensity and transparency. The Silk Roads provide a universal medium through which geopolitical, economic, and socio-political aspirations can be expressed, transmitted, critiqued, and sometimes even realized.

The revival of the Silk Roads in contemporary discourse reflects a recognition of their historical role in fostering global connections. The Belt and Road Initiative (BRI), launched by China, is a prime example of how the legacy of the Silk Roads continues to influence modern global infrastructure and economic projects. The BRI aims to enhance connectivity and cooperation across Eurasia, mirroring the ancient Silk Roads' role in facilitating trade and cultural exchange.

Globalization, driven by technological advancements and increased interconnectivity, has reshaped the world in ways that parallel the impact of the Silk Roads. Just as the Silk Roads facilitated the exchange of goods, ideas, and cultures, modern globalization promotes the flow of information, technology, and cultural practices across borders. The digital revolution has created new "information superhighways" that connect people and societies in real-time, echoing the ancient trade routes' role in bridging distant regions.

Moreover, the Silk Roads have become a powerful symbol of resilience and adaptability in the face of change. Despite the collapse of empires and the shifting political landscapes, the trade routes adapted and persisted, continuing to facilitate exchanges across Eurasia. This adaptability is mirrored in modern globalization, where societies continually evolve and adapt to new economic and technological realities.

In conclusion, the Silk Roads serve as a potent symbol for modern globalization, embodying the principles of connectivity, exchange, and adaptability. By understanding their historical significance, we can gain insights into the processes that shape our contemporary world. The legacy of the Silk Roads reminds us of the enduring importance of global connections in fostering economic prosperity, cultural exchange, and mutual understanding.

CHAPTER 16

Conclusion

The story of the Silk Roads and their intricate interactions across the top of the world represents one of the crucial nerve endings of human history. Throughout this book, I hope to have emphasized the vital importance of the Silk Roads in our understanding and appreciation of ancient trade networks' role in shaping our civilizations on a broad, truly global scale. These routes served as the intracivilizational system of exchange, connecting monarchs, merchants, and everyone in between, thereby acting as the lifeblood of ancient Asia.

Silk, which ignited global interest in the 300s AD, transformed the ancient world. Asia has continued to function like the linguistic equivalent of the Silk Roads, communicating with its "ancient" neighbors in ways that differ fundamentally from the predominantly intra-European exchanges of the last 500 years. The Silk Roads facilitated not only the movement of goods but also the flow of ideas, culture, and knowledge, creating a dynamic network that enriched and influenced civilizations far and wide.

The perspective of the Silk Roads is crucial for understanding our modern debates regarding globalization. As we navigate the complexities of contemporary global interactions, the lessons from the Silk Roads provide valuable insights. These ancient trade routes highlight the significance of interconnectivity and the exchange of ideas in fostering economic prosperity and cultural enrichment.

Examining the chain of interactions across Eurasia reveals the deep historical roots of concepts such as the "Renaissance" and "modern" values, which date back at least fifteen hundred years. It is hardly surprising that Enlightenment thinkers drew inspiration from Asia, as civilizations under silk's influence flourished with innovation and creativity. The legacy of the Silk Roads reminds us that our present is deeply intertwined with our past, an "entangled bank" of evolution linking our systems of globalization in ways that are both profound and intricate.

In conclusion, the Silk Roads offer a compelling narrative of how ancient trade networks shaped the course of human history. By understanding their legacy, we gain a greater appreciation for the interconnectedness of our world and the enduring impact of these routes on globalization. As we move forward, the lessons from the Silk Roads can guide us in fostering a more interconnected and prosperous future, reminding us that our past continues to influence our present and shape our destiny.

www.ingramcontent.com/pod-product-compliance
Lightning Source LLC
Chambersburg PA
CBHW051502140726
47987CB00006B/2846